Praise for *Heaven with Oth*

Barbara Molloy's new collection *Heaven with Others* is a feast for the senses, as well as an elegiac reminder that all we have is the present. These poems study mortality: "As if it was not her at all,/dying,/ about to die,/being dead,/or returned to life…" ("Gift of Sunflowers"). In the hands of this accomplished lyricist even the most sordid past is rendered as fine art and gifted with visceral re-birth in organic images not easily forgotten: "Leaves strewn about the yards--/the exact color of church and rectory bricks…" (Breeze). Molloy's voice brings down the high-brow and lifts up the colloquial. We are the beneficiaries of her vision.
—Judith Skillman

In this new collection, Barbara Molloy Olund keeps a sharp focus on the chaos of discarded objects and lives while tracking surprising moments of humor. "Who said 'cherish the moments' and/ 'life gives you a lemon; make lemonade?'/ Are they tired yet?…" asks the narrator (Of Ghosts). These poems respect the hard work of living. There's an intention here, almost a promise, to never let go of what matters, no matter how seemingly unimportant an object or detail, how elusive a relationship—what prevails is the intention to continue searching for what's real and what's not. "I will not love the past./ Let it glitter. Let it sit forward…" (Decision). I admire how this work confronts the spiritual labor of care giving, birthing, struggling with addiction, negotiating with ghosts, and parenting. And I'm touched by the ongoing, archetypal process running through these pages—the sorting-out of wisps of beauty from the detritus of life.
—Christianne Balk

Heaven with Others

Barbara Molloy

Červená Barva Press
Somerville, Massachusetts

Červená Barva Press
P.O. Box 440357
W. Somerville, MA 02144-3222

www.cervenabarvapress.com

Bookstore: www.thelostbookshelf.com

Cover Art: "Sunflowers," by Barbara Molly, 2022, pencil and acrylic on paper, 12" x 14"

Cover Design: William J. Kelle

ISBN: 978-1-950063-54-3

Library of Congress Control Number: 2023930901

ACKNOWLEDGMENT

This book would not be possible without the incredible generosity and keen insights of poet and artist, Judith Skillman.

TABLE OF CONTENTS

I.

II.

III.

For Peter Olund: Jan. 8, 1990 - May 6, 2018

He cannot tell the rate at which he travels backwards.

—Elizabeth Bishop, *The Man-Moth*

Heaven with Others

1.

Fire Whispered

The warehouse will be ash.
Beams become one,
flares scorched out.
The sky will go orange to pink to sherbet,
then smoke-blacked,
dulled to haze, pall, and paler ash.

Addresses, doors, windows, cross-beams,
planters—everything not combustible
will be seared.
The letters WELCOME
singed to the door mat.
The other side of the lake as light as noon.
The moon obscure, its candle wax
dripping into water.

My uncle's A-frame cedar,
do it yourself—gone.
We said grace over dinner
at the home-made table.
Bowing my head to pray, passing the bowl
of bacon-flecked potatoes.

Auntie was her quiet self.
More ham, potatoes? How's school?
It looks like champagne,
my fire, a geyser blooming from a boot.

Next, sirens wailing
like wolves imitating sirens.
It's time for the sleeping to wake,
for the easily greased to sit up.

I'm down in the basement
finishing up algebra—unable to sleep,
myself on fire—
when he comes into the room to tell me
what I already know.

Moon of the Salamanders
  After finding a picture of cows in a second-hand bookstore

The thaw's just lifting
the marsh up to the spring rains.
On its jetty of leaf, the salamander—

with its slick, avid, witty face,
goes "bob-bobbing away."
Luck returns like vanishing

streams. By page eighteen
they're safe, your cows.
I want you to know how safe they are.

The spotted one, and the other:
drab-colored, a lick
of cud still dangling. My son

recognized their importance
right away and placed their photo
on his mantle—the windowsill—

between the dead battery,
beetle's carapace, shells, and sticks.
If you love them, please know

they're loved now by accident.
He collects all good things at this age,
of which there are too many.

He's constantly shifting. The claw
of a Dungeness Crab withers,
begins to stink before he relents,

putting it behind the split
broom handle.
He's like a man interested

at least as much in the order
of his ledger as the bottom line,
someone who might one day say:

"My greatest regret?
That's for hindsight to conclude, yet
I write to inform you the world is shrinking."

But you know this. You posed
your two cows in the photo
he tried not to fold or crush.

Noticing it was already beginning
to fade and tear,
he shoved it hastily

into the page that read:
"It tapped. It purled.
But the salamander

loved rain. Each torrent
of water was transportation."
In the background, three trailers,

blue and aluminum. A sapling
in the foreground, wrapped
like a sprain. Were you selling

your cows before the year
thinned entirely? They peer
at us like dark-eyed sisters

recently in touch, posing
under eaves of a beer garden.
And the salamander?

"When a rivulet of water washed
over him, he would be picked up."
I write to say the world

is shrinking—
yes, but not before
you fatten it up. Name it Lucky,

Buddy or Snowface, and don't forget
to love it enough to wander off,
if just for a moment.

Sandwich and Institution

in memory of my father

Now you're quiet
in the apartment inside
a gated yard at twilight.
Across the way, children screech
under a beach-ball descending,
scatter like Jays.

You're turning the key
on a can of sardines,
hunching over a map
of Florida. A TV flashes
in the background.

You hear the neighbor,
Esther, usually bent over shuffle-board.
Nice, but "a tad talky"—
—the same Esther
who once made
you a sandwich,
tap at your window screen.

You feign sleep.
She knocks harder.
It's hot. You're polite
as she hands you yet
another sandwich.

This is not the sandwich
you remember,
nor the sandwich you dreamed.

Decision

I will not love the past.
Let it glitter. Let it sit forward.
I will not have a wild eye
threatening to crowd me
out of myself.

I'll walk into the bar.
Velvet seats, candles—
or call it a pub—sad anachronism
with juke box and sticky benches
resembling pews.

I'll lift my face to order,
have a white wine, thinking Bloody Mary.
I'll wink back at the first man who turns
on his stool to acknowledge me
as I look but do not feel mercurial.

Let reality grow disenchanted
with me. Like autumn—
a dash of color here, leaves go gold
there. They gather at the curb.
They fall inside the body first,

leaves. Attach my sadness
to theirs—bone marrow, shadow, wisps of hair.
I'll lock my hand around
a wine stem and be terrified
of being afraid. Is the mist

outside light? Can the beefy arms
of some stranger who isn't
even flirting anymore
be wrapped round me
even as I recede?

Rubbish Day

They'd stand at the curb. She,
dressed for the Russian Winter. He,
the husband,
stooping gingerly.
They had to know by feel.

Think of the bat's blind scanning of fields,
as he put his hand down and down
into our trash. Always to come up
with something.
Our kitchen curtains, for example.

She, the woman, spread them out
on her knees like a map.
Yellowed, cigarette stained,
yet recently cleaned and still pleated.
There was the pile

that went with them—to keep—
in the truck's back
and the pile they left on the curb.
Old as me now, she's opening her coat
to receive things: unfinished color books,

mismatched gloves,
an ashtray in the shape of an airplane—
Delta Logo. Fake goldfish
in a fake plastic bowl.
Comics, Nancy Drew paperbacks, aluminum, wax.

He'd frisk the outer layers
with the same hand—
stand back, wipe his palm on his sleeve,
before bending down.
Sometimes his hand would come up empty—

like a fish surprised at the air
it snaps. There was efficiency

in how he'd wipe each item
on his sleeve first
before handing it off to the woman

who waited and then took it in or put it back.

Of Ghosts

My old man's put two angels made of crepe
and pipe-cleaners over a cardboard diorama
manger. Baby Christ, cardboard also,
reaches scrubby arms up.

He asks me to get him a drink.
I'm a waiter in Chicago
serving vodka straight up.

Mary and Joseph need paint.
The ledge over the door
holds a fading cornucopia
donated by local public #108.

I love the impossible transition
known as season.
I shut my car door,
cross the soft tarred parking lot
surrounded by bedraggled Oaks,
Elms, Maples stamping the ground with last colors.
Push the buzzer—let myself in

His face ensconced in covers
lights up. "Darling," he ekes out
before his eyes close again.

I'd like to steal us a couple
ciggies, pour him a vodka,
throw the window open—
invite Cal the janitor
who's out there by the dumpsters
right now rolling his own on a break.

Who said "cherish the moments" and
"life gives you a lemon; make lemonade?"
Are they tired yet?

Decision

The past's wet eye sits forward. I walk into the bar,
sit down in a velvety booth lit cozy by a cherubic candle.

Alright, call it a pub, booze-sticky,
anachronistic, juke-box-shadow of itself—
benches from a condemned church—and lift my face to order.

"White wine" I say
as I wink back at the first man
turning his swivel chair to acknowledge me.

Whoever you are letting reality grow disenchanted
just now when I'm feeling so and secure,

you allowing autumn to spill so much color
it's blasphemy to tread on the leaves;

all the leaves being the one that fell inside my body first—
Who are you,
Fist curled round my wine-stem?

Sure. After a couple sips
we're feeling so one the baddest
country music's a hymn I sway to forgetting
I'm not flirting anymore.

But Tenderly

She had something they couldn't cure
which naming would make only more elusive.
She had a cucumber-colored bathroom
with towels folded in such a way
you could wipe your hands
without spoiling the triangular fold.
Like pulling a gift out of its paper
without mussing the wrap.

I cleaned the whole apartment,
beginning at the bathroom's porcelain
and ending, depending on the day,
at the door of the microwave, gleaming.
The shades remained drawn
regardless the time of day
as she supervised from bed.

She scared me most when quiet.
I'd wish she'd wake
and shush me for humming.
Or sit up, an eighty-year-old patient,
her wig scantily attached to her scalp
like the lampshade to its light.

Then she'd orchestrate again
how I should dust the elephant plant
leaf by leaf with a cotton cloth
and spray bottle.

I still see her hands folded on top
of the bed covers.
How the light outside,
greedy for itself,
would slip through the shade's slats
so that as she fell back—
click—a disembodied whistle from her teeth—
she'd fallen asleep this time
completely, her head ensconced on the pillow.

She

Each time I come into the room
I bring him a new child.
I don't have time for inspections,
to answer all the questions I hear
him ask in my mind.

Why does it always look up? Why
prefer rivers to birds? Where
are its teeth, and what have
you done with the others?
Etcetera. We had

had a past. Then, one
day I ached for a child.
One bright eyed, soft baby—
no-bigger-than-a-cake-child.
Soon, I continued to make them.

He would insist they weren't ours, mine...
"That's just an old milk bottle,"
he'd say. "That's just a train
going by." You can imagine
how quiet I'd become

even as I sang the same song
over and over till I caused a pity
to grow in his eye. I would just sing,
or brush up against something
and a tender infant would appear.

What would we do with all
of them? Then, how long before
they wanted out, craved
moonlight, burst onto pavement
like an old tavern song

while I sat alone in the same room—
knitting by television light,

polishing silver. He said,
"You'd have let everything into
your body in time."

After Some Soft Porn with Barn Theme

After rain, dull heat, rain,
a downpour tearing the sky open
like a sack of grain.
Rust devours a sitting plow
just shy of the abandoned field,
its orange heart-shaped shiny-as-Jupiter-seat.
They undress in phases—
quarter crescent to half moon—
to keep the eye moving, as the eye is a scavenger.
A sack of flour, a bale of hay.
I'm a sucker for it all—clean lines,
pictures over words, airbrushed.
Voluptuous skin, soft lighting
mimicking dusk.

The barn is well cast. Collapsed,
swallowing itself in an ark of ribs
on a Sunday drive in Decatur,
the smell of manure turned
by a machine only once removed
from the oxen it replaced.
Meanwhile the farmer's gone—
forced to sell everything. His barn's
flat side is billboard space
reading: Drink Coca Cola.

When the pretty "daughter"
goes down on the out-of-towner—
a handsome yet rough hewn trucker who got lost
en route, light seeps through the rafters.
She removes her bra, one strap
at a time, having dropped her frilly blouse.
And he, pants pooled at his feet,
buttocks exposed to shadows,
moonlight dampened—he offers up
an even more perfect globe,

the baby's head
emerging from swaddling
like cabbage or swine.

11.

The Virgin

Because we didn't have
a beach, she was our Sea.
Her oval face
proffered quietly
while the rest
of her stood
upright—one foot
rooted but soft in front
of the other.

A floodlight from behind
lit her up. Always the gate
clanged or winced.

Behind, a dip in the asphalt
letting leaves blow in,
hither & thither.
After curfew, me and Steve
slipped inside the roped-off edge.

Like a Great Wall,
her veil, fluted
to the hem,
where it all dropped
away suddenly,
the floor of an ocean.

I put my plastic cup
full of cheap gin
on the pedestal
floating her gentle feet.
He laid his dull green
army coat over the wet ground.
These places
are our true houses.

Stones, a mossy ledge.
Looking up

I could easily guess
I was not supposed to leave
this place or him, ever,
have a past, never mind
grow weathered myself
as a beam in a house
when in fact I was the same.

I picture her to this day
arms ensconced in robe folds,
palms clasped in a prayer
that includes me,
the cynic ascending.

In Beauty In Drag

When she looked at me, the man
who was a woman who was among friends
at a table in a Thai restaurant—
a card table, nothing fancy mind you—
I admit I was put off.

They were all in drag ten or twelve friends
that crisp October night.
She the more glam of them.
High cheekbones, wavy hair, a tall drink of water,
even sitting and well turned out,
as my mother, a lover of fashion herself,
would have noted.

Petite marshmallow earrings,
twinkly strands, a white
shell-neck sweater pinched
at the shoulders collecting her mole-dotted
cleavage. They ordered the big share plates,
vegetables drowning in sauces red
and green. Swimming Rhama.

There was a Buddha in an alcove
behind the host station
where water dripped a simulation
of water dripping into a well.
I don't know what the 'look'
was. Not the look a man gives a
woman but shy of?

I did what I'd have done if she was a man—
gaze away from, then towards
the carp circling
in their murky tank.

The other scenario?
I'd have kept my eyes on the fish

for the few seconds flirtation requires,
and then looked back at him.

Gift of Sunflowers and the Woman Who Crossed Over

I know no guardian in tunic
waits to pull me gently from the wreck,
wings cumbersome and sleek
as the moon-tinged guardrail.

I understand too, there's no soul to sport
my soul individually from death,
the thing itself, its extra curriculum,
recedes like weight
while the moment still spins
inside.

She was dead. She knew she was
dead, the woman who "crossed over."
Her only witness herself, aside from the TV
interviewer, was me.

It was that same afternoon, mid-October, my friend
gave me sunflowers, several
she'd cut and arranged—
if you can make them a bouquet, sunflowers,
or handsome.
You know how it is
with gifts? These
top heavy, awkward, already drooping,
spilling their pollen.

I felt as if I'd been given to them.
I found a zinc tub, the only vessel to fit—stuck them in,
left them in water on my deck,
the sun going down, their silhouettes

reminiscent of bathers in the 30's
who can only wade out shallowly
for the heavy skirts bundled in
their fists.

When she was returned, the woman said,

to life, she cried out:
"put me back; I am; I was, I'm—dead!"
Because she had seen a light
that had called her eye
and it had been more beautiful
than anything else
she'd seen in life.

From her strange perspective
a few minutes, seconds
she could watch, see, the flitting about her, down below,
of hospital staff, nurses and attendants—
adjusting her position for comfort, replenishing IV's
as she lay on the gurney below
herself splayed out softly in
a pale hospital gown.

And how they pushed—
two nurses in tandem, on her sternum
pressing down once, and again, not unlike she'd pressed
on the Volkswagen's horn
seconds before she was "taken."

Next she was coughing
on her own breath, sitting up
in the bed. Like something
"kick-started," "a spark blown back in
through a window," albeit sobbing.

Her name was Vivien.
The doctors could only tell her
how long she'd been
gone before she "came to."

Meanwhile, I had my own sunflowers,
a row of them in the yard, flopping
over the garbage tins, leaving seeds the crows
and other varmints scattered
off drunk on.

They're too big, sunflowers,
to be flowers. Five feet some,
mammalian. The season
lies down in each—bole, petal, leaf and stem—
like an old horse going blind,
put out to pasture.

They beg for personification:
a dirge or a fight song,
this harvest curled into its last leaves,
bruised pumpkins, tomato rot,
flies, bees, pulp. An apple
drops at the slightest nudge
of wind. "A firestorm of brain chemicals"
said the neurologist.

As if it was not her at all,
dying, about to die, being dead,
or returned to life,
rather a collision of otherwise discreet
processes no one doctor or scientist
could have foreseen.

She now believed in heaven,
a light she could no more touch than enter
as she heard the one night nurse
say to the other
"Where's Ruthie…I'm off at ten."

Bathing Muriel

I'd lift one withered arm up, scrub it,
and then the other. She'd squirm,
start midway through to become flimsy.
Inevitably, she'd slip, loosen her grip,
set her arm down limp on the sponge
till I blundered. Then it was soap in her eyes,
water on the floor. She'd scream, Get me my towel!

I was told to not grow indispensable.
There were boundaries. There was a time frame.
Often I'd pretend a distance, as though arriving
at her apartment for the first time. I'd notice
a new sheen to her kitchen: how yellow the yellow.

Once she'd put a poem up with a nephew's
picture on the refrigerator using the decorative
magnets of flowering cactus we'd bought.
So much was like the view of the lake she had
from her kitchen window. Even her condition.

Sometimes the choppy grey water,
both neutral and rough, was most apparent.
Next minute, the water was turquoise and smoother
than the base of her crystal bowl
posing with fake fruit on a card table—
or the whole place from the kitchen outward
could glow in a violent sunset.

I recall, after a letter from her sister,
Muriel embraced me suddenly.
I was tired that day and only held on politely.
Then one day I arrived to find
her walking the hallway naked.
I covered her with my sweatshirt,
drawing her inside with the lie that we
would go for ice-cream if she dressed.

There was always a next time.
I arrived and she held the vacuum
hose to her hair. What are you doing?
I said snapping the plug.
You've been gone three days. I'm filthy, she screamed.

Strangely, she'd cleaned. The apartment was spotless,
the baseboards and places I'd never touched,
windows and windowpanes too clean.
As if she'd been swabbing
for three nights with ammonia and bleach.

By then she couldn't stand at all. I could see
through her skin past her bones—
her ankles purple and swelling.
She shook like the last winter leaf,
and still asked, because every day
is a new day, could we go out for ice cream.

Cow in the Distance

This cow causes all the waste. Mud-splotched milk
cow. No precedent, lying

there in labor, on a dry mud-flat. You can't dream up labor
or garbage either, wet pieces, silty cakes

or any broad field of unabashed returnables,
plastic or wooden table legs. And

you can't go back to when the function
was alone, itself, without form.

You can't go back although you know
how it used to be. A headache ballooning

towards the corpus of its relief
could be suffered for a while, whereas

everyone knew there was an end
without an "off button." Aren't we everyone we dream?

Over a gradation, a slope
of eggshell, dead batteries and vegetable rot,

sulfurous miasma that could "go up in an instant."
Aren't we the someone in the next

apartment, lighting a candle, reading
the guide book about fortune as its opposite?

Darling Institution

What saved me was obligatory grounds
where I'd stroll. I imagined myself "on location"
or the contrary—in concrete reality.

The grass, roll-out sod—landscaping
tended by Mexicans: a beautiful benign mixture
of indigenous and exotics where a butterfly
might still land. The parking lot
hidden by flora, like varicose
under a lampshade.

There was a television, thank goodness.
On all day or night, with its remote handy
to all. I could watch it or not,
be reminded either way by its glare
what a slight change in routine
it is to be insane.

It was the picture of paradise in the
common room that kept me up:
scared, going, awake.

The night nurse would come in
with two capsules, a glass of water or juice
on the stand she'd roll in immediately out. .
Juice tumbler, FM radio, and ashtray.
I stared and stared at the snake.
I felt sorry for it. Ensconced on the slimmer
portion of tree trunk I'd determined
was Eve's ankle. An audience
is one thing, an audience of one, another.

What about the snake's little shrunken purse
of a face staring at me?
Did it want something? When coiled,
it's still slick. Wrapped around muscle
or branch, tail-touching its own beginning,

31

A man spilled his drink on me at the opening.
I remember thinking the real garden
was the whole dampened ward
of us sleeping. We're guests, too.

I got up, stepped into my hospital
slippers, went to the mirror.
Alright, I need faith, or the thing
that sets it apart from us.
I looked closely at my face.
I still cling to it in some way, too, not unlike the theater.

I rub oil into my features,
rings in my neck. Dear little Eve
or Adam—I've been Cleopatra,
Maria, Louisa, Jane.

I've been all but the snake in my smoke,
snake in my drink, my neck,
partners and extras, my arthritic fingers.
I've been a hand come out of nowhere
in the subway one evening when I left
my flat without combing my hair.

Wrapped round the southern portion
of one blue eternal tree, finest actor.
Yet a snake is a snake manages nothing
outside its calling. Me?
I'm an actress.
I crave applause.

Prayer for Boomtown Angels

Dearest winged desires outside.
Your face resting on wings. You—
sweet cabbage wrapped in petals cherubs.
Waxy fruits, you enfants under whom
we browse the European Bread Section—
I don't think we care how you mend. Just do.
Loves come apart. Death surveys from its stoop.

Snag us like trout in the talons of an otherwise
Placid night. Spirituous,
Appear over snow bleared meadows
silent screens of televisions buried. Shape shift
time. Float the calm.
Peruse us—the contents of the purse—
of the life we've been given, believe us as
only you can. We believe in you.
Dive bomb the crease in fat, furl the tunnel's end—
dark pouring light. Be the slate,
wipe clean the median we're alone with at night undressing.

Bear us the bridge, smile from electric currents,
wink from waste water. Brush the tear in the curtain,
draft the hiccup. Call us by name, anyone's.
Vivien, Hank, Thelonius. Know it all, forget and repeat
with a purpose for years stared into. Hatch, reach, repeal
cabins and children. Reduce infinity. Change the math, locks,
the game itself. Go further if you must.
One kidney, bursitis and a broken broom.
Lend notes, heave sorrow from a spoon.
Compare us in shame to materials we waste, gossip, exaggerate.
Hear us—white space waiting in line in box stores,
racket dispersing into crickets chirping for mates.
Fall us from grace quoting sanity's billboard: Two for one. Jesus
saves.
Jump the headline: Fiery Crash.
Then come back once more as the man or woman

33

pulled from the wreck, placed again into the great
peace you've conducted involuntarily all these years
from a fog of gnats treading a chair beside the bean plants.

No More Melissa

It keeps streaming
from the device
and I'm tired of it: love,
the old unrequited.
I'm as tired as the old

roll-up window of this obsolete
car, stripped
to where I've got duct tape
on the passenger side
keeping out the elements.

It keeps howling–
love, the wind, ruminations, threading
and rethreading the same
theme: I'm alone.
I understand.

I'm driving groceries
home—onions, cheese
and an oversize jug
of laundry detergent,
which, when I turn, leans

against my arm.
Melissa. Always
your name, Melissa.
Capable of a lilt,
then an arc into screech.

The sudden refrain
dissolving into percussion
like vapor. When I push
on the defrost
ice marbles the road edge.

An opossum leaps past
my brights into a ditch.

Possum frisking cellophane.
Who is this man
awash in the hard

jarring rhythms of Melissa—
the one who keeps
the place always
one person awake—
raw, hoarse, heartbroken.

Heaven with Others

Bingo. Crazy 8's. This on a 3x5
note card: try more egg white in devil's food
cake. Francine's hand—Francine? Gone,

gone. Heaven? Heaven
will replace us
with its own profundities—

discerning that autumn
or spring wasted casually
while the trouble of life kept turning

over incidentals, like leaves.
Foisting children on us
and then retreating.

What does Harquebus mean?
Or the foul-breathed cat who used to frisk
the screens of lower windows toppling

my cucumber cactus—
what was its name? Rudy, Rudolph? A word
is manna from Heaven:

Brigitte, Esther, Rutherford—gone, as gone
as those pancakes I poured water on
in my dreams.

God bless us all.
What is 7x9? If I remember
I wake, pierced by what my mind

conjures instead.
The sunroom! Why am I
standing in the sunroom?

I haven't been standing
in the sunroom
for years.

111.

Letter to Hawk Enthusiast

Hen's blood on the wind—Goshawk,
that nice stripe of moonlight
slicing its eye—
wends up from the pond.
My wife joins me.
We watch it place its prey
on the stoop. We wait.

The bald eye isn't orange
as the guidebook indicates,
rather, yellow. It glowers
like a cataract.
The famous wingspan,
a great hingeless door
reveals legs sturdy in a pad
of feathers—chaps.

I'm writing this now—
having never written
your journal before,
having been an avid reader,
to say my wife and I
were sleeping
when we heard the thud.

I envisioned Mallards
overhead the property
we've been building
for a lifetime
among Cedar and Douglas Fir.

Right now, sickle moon
in a slight gap
reflects cameo-like
where the pond feeds
into a creek.
Naive as I am
and sleepy, I imagine a situation

where two birds career
midair. Sometimes
the most impossible
variables line up.

For instance, one afternoon
two geese collided.
I found them bloodied
and flopped
among our crazed chickens.
Does the Goshawk mate for life, like some?

I've lived under a few roofs,
as many migrations.
But this time, what
landed on my doorstep—its profile

so much like the specimen
in your magazine,
that I—sans binoculars
yet considering myself
a professor of nature—
am compelled to write.

Dead Duck

Neck twisted,
beak a brilliant yellow—
jabs at the street.
Visible eye,
out-turned
looks up,
into, forward
toward flight.

The duck feels
alive here,
in this peaceful
place from which
flight's been lifted.

The sky's dull,
not blue or grey,
a blank haze
waiting distillation
on this day. Day
of the dead
duck on a side-street.

Blood leaves
a faint trail of
grease between
stones. Duck as cause
or duck as effect?
Some time elapses
before decay
when still vital, moist,
splayed instead
of splattered—
vibrantly striped
—the neck,
however broken
is as if painted
teal, black

and white,
perfectly still—
when death
appears to be sleeping.

A blow
too keen to be random,
inside itself,
put it here—duck
not far
from dust
of an overpass.
Waxy decoy
of duck, dead,
a joke
is buried in
here, somewhere, I'd
think, like guilt glided
deftly around
in every dream
where the witness
is also perceiver.

Beady eyed, bald,
web-footed,
left alone to waft
or raft
above house,
creek, summer
lodge—no less
obscure when dead
than any
shiny item
found and left
unburied
and relieved.

It's Only Weather

It's been years since a wind as big
as this one, says the man after the hurricane.
An old timer, he's relishing the details
for an interviewer.

As form follows function,
so his bathroom floated
into history. And he could see
from the drowned shore those fixtures
he'd nailed to a wall, his towel
hanging off the rack he'd made
and pounded into tiles.

He could all but touch them—
towel and rack and light fixture—
the whole damn bathroom
bobbing away from him
like a telephone booth
navigating whitewater
while remaining intact.

There's things we haven't seen yet
that compared to the things
we've seen make us feel small, he said.
I have no idea what that means
but I believe him.

He lost everything
in an unforeseen accident of weather.
It happens elsewhere, the moment
that makes the last moment seem
trivial. Trees swoon, a metal wire buzzes,
pigeons startle, who can think
of sleeping? A woman carries a chair inside
that would otherwise have flown away.

Erstwhile Vacation

Otherwise, just a horse-shoe coast,
bigger than most,
fairly unspoiled by my American
eye. Wispy, no less palpable
stars, like the pithier
fruits, climbing down swayback branches
from the pitch-dark sky.

I'm telling my mum, just go!
Take the damn French lessons—
she's curled in blankets
in front of television.

Smiling too gently,
so that it's me on her case
and no litany of excuses,
saying no one cares if you get
in the car right now.
Drive, or don't.
She's falling all the more comfortably
back into her eggroll.

I wish I knew how
they got here, lovers. I'm in
my suit, holding
my towel—a bottle of House
Chard in a wax cup,
about to swim out alone
past the buoy. I hear them
before I see them,
holding one another
floating back-to-stomach to-back, feet
(a man's?) flip propeller-like.

They're like otters, the darkness spits
them quietly up again.
Umpteen ways to turn my head
but I don't. Next,

I see the volley-ball
net, a tired web attached to sinking poles
beside a native tree—
what is the name of that fruit?

If I can skim the landscape
with my eye—
get up without acknowledging
the swimming or
floating back-to-stomach-to-back—
a button will not be pushed,
an insult won't happen.
Something pure will be forgotten.

It's as if it's looking at me—
that moon-like fruit
perched in the crook
of a native tree.
Otherwise, just a horse-shoe coast,
bigger than most,
fairly unspoiled by my American eye.

I wish I knew how
they got here, lovers. I'm in
my suit, holding
my towel—
a bottle of House
Chardonnay, a wax cup,
about to swim out alone
past the buoy—
I hear them before I see
them—holding one another
in an embrace.

Self Portrait: Mother and Van Gogh

Longtime tomatoes and roses have fallen
like color from his arm.
She'd have been lying at home
with the television
exploding into cheerfulness—
my mum—so I took her out.

It's always Van Gogh. No matter
how they arrange the periods
in corridors, rooms of ignored
women, sculptures.

Careful to leave enough white space
between, we wind up back
at him. She can stand in front
of Van Gogh forever,
or Degas' ballerinas.

Meanwhile, she'll complain
she didn't want to go
in the first place
if we stop in front of a piece
that "leaves the earth" too much.

"Maybe the artist wanted us to think,"
I say when she stops
in front of a big white
canvas sliced in half by one ink stripe.

"I don't want to think!" she snaps.
Later, we eat chicken salad
in the cafeteria.
Above us, somewhere between a skylight
and the ceiling, a pigeon's gotten
trapped. Pecking and scratching.

"Look," she says.
It starts just then

to snow the kind of white first flakes
that make the pigeon seem dirty,
but which would be ashen by the time
we got to our car, as it was Chicago.

So I ask "have you even called
about the insulation yet?"
She can't say.
"This is Chicago. Winter!"
I try not to raise my voice.
When her whole face and body shrink,
I only curse and let it in.

I tell her what shoes to wear,
show her how to align
the numbers in the checkbook
inside the columns.
I pretend for both of us that this is simple.

"Then there is the other idle man,
who is idle in spite of himself, who
is inwardly consumed by a great
longing for action,"
That would be Van Gogh.

After circling
the parking garage on foot,
we go back in to fetch her purse.
By then her corns are acting up
so I leave her alone
beside the elevator.

On a bench nearby,
when I come back down
she's sitting peacefully.

Then, as we step outside,
arm in arm,
she says, "reach right through you,
those stars, don't they?"

Breeze

It comes back.
A day like this one—
late August or September.
As though the breeze stirred
itself from the anachronism
of my Catholic heart.

The schoolyard
flag is flapping
on its sage pole in a dry wind.
Leaves strewn about the yards:
the exact color
of church and rectory bricks.

Inside, rooms
of sweat and ammonia.
Desks are over, rows
we sat in, like words:
listen, repeat, stand up,
and you may be seated.

That's why I'm
sad for a minute, and then,
like the weather, it's gone.

In detention,
early that Bible?—
so old a film ruined me
after I secretly lifted and turned
its first pages—no one was looking.

I put it back
on the shelf, where old crayons,
the ones halved and snapped
by pressing too hard
were collected in a tin.

This tin not far
from another book about
a ballerina I could never
forget who was compelled
to dance forever, spinning away
on red toe shoes, infinitely
far from her own little town.

Flight of Geese on Television

They go over like enchanted mail—
a long train
we're exempt from.

They skim the night
of blue-black clouds,
multiplying in tandem overhead.

The lullaby of sheep counted one by one,
the sheep we resist metaphorically.
Like lemmings, because we are them.

A feast rests inside
a nut. There is a point
to the geese, but it's not what we think.

After a scant rain, they arrive
slower—dip, slant, split.
Re-weave. The night is purple but green,

multiplied by stars and far off.
Is it their genius to never
be finished with their unbroken chain,

their trail, train, arrow, ribbon, wake?
En route from Canada,
On Nova, December of 1994—

he'll be five in a month—
my son when the *V* he points to in recognition
is them, the geese exactly like those

over our raking the other day when he asked "Are ducks geese?"
Who thinks these distinctions up?
They sweep across our field of view.

New inventions can't hold them:
the toggle, contrast, zoom, neural net, VR,

and other things we'll fiddle with until the next one,

flightless ourselves, easily distracted.
At the same time, their honks sound
like we're leaving them.

Movies, the Sequel

There's more blood in this one.
Splattered across a shirt.
Carpet as beautiful and corrupt
as the deepest rose appearing all of a sudden
in the height of summer.

Veins and valves, which make us
love the lip of fat and the stem
and that which gives meat its milk.
It's the mouth ourselves, the same bit
we slice off rather than eat.

In this way Cinema is all but merciful,
to give me to feel in the dark as I sit back
on an arc in a plush seat
while the body on-screen is pumped
full of bullets.

It twitches, taking a few steps
toward and away impact.
In his apartment before falling,
blood trailing
like petals. The big cheese falls

against the standing lamp,
a hole in his white shirt
They haven't finished painting
his apartment. Now he lies there,
slack-mouthed, galled, right eye twitching.

Beside a coffee table, magazines,
and a glass he held just before
he was spilled guts, his pinky held
jealously out—blown wire, derailed branch
petal connecting him to this life.

Although it was not a good
movie, nevertheless, blood lingers

jewel-like, rises above
its own surface in a clot
or thrombosis or pool as red as forever.

Recurrent Cows

These lazy cows cause all the waste.
They lie down on some slope
after eating into the depression that was grass.

They are indifferent as the moles
dotting their undersides,
dumb as the fallopian splotches

distinguishing their herds.
Whoever's given birth is forsaking
and forgiving of their alma mater thereafter.

Who dreams this up? Abundance
gnashing cud. Naïve, quietest of beasts.
One word—moooooooooo—contains everything.

Even while birthing, no—especially then—
they ask nothing, like day or sky.
Real girth isn't moody.

Once, the fittest Jersey gave out, collapsing on table-legs
to give her calf up to the earth like a wet corsage.
As if much could arise out of nothing.

ABOUT THE AUTHOR

Barbara Molloy is a writer, artist, and jazz vocalist who makes her home in Coupeville, Washington on beautiful Whidbey Island. A previous book of poems, *In Favor of Lightning*, was published by Wesleyan University Press. Ms. Molloy's work has been nominated for Pushcart prizes and has won awards from The Pen Foundation. Her poems have appeared in a variety of literary journals.